MᴄKɪɴɴᴇʏ Fᴀʟʟs

McKinney Falls

The Ranch Home of Thomas F. McKinney,
Pioneer Texas Entrepreneur

By Margaret Swett Henson

Texas State
Historical Association

Library of Congress Cataloging-in-Publication Data

Henson, Margaret Swett, 1924–
   McKinney Falls: The Ranch Home of Thomas F. McKinney, Pioneer Texas
   Entrepreneur / by Margaret Swett Henson
      p.   cm.   —(Fred Rider Cotten popular history series; no. 12
   Includes bibliographical references.
   ISBN 0-87611-172-X
   1. McKinney Homestead (Austin, Tex.) 2. Austin Region (Tex.)—Buildings,
   structures, etc. 3. Austin Region (Tex.)—Biography. 4. McKinney, Thomas
   Freeman, 1801–1871—Homes and haunts—Texas—Austin Region. 5.
   Pioneers—Texas—Austin Region—Biography. 7. Ranches—Texas—Austin
   Region—History—19th century. 8. McKinney Falls State Park (Tex.)—History.
   I. Title. II. Series.
   F394.A98M384   1999
   976.4'31—dc21
                                                                        99-51738
                                                                        CIP

Published by the Texas State Historical Association in cooperation with the Center
for Studies in Texas History at the University of Texas at Austin.

Cover: McKinney Falls. Photograph by Greg White courtesy Texas Department of
Transportation.

CONTENTS

INTRODUCTION

MCKINNEY FALLS STATE PARK in Austin is about six miles southeast of the state capitol. It lies south of Ben White Boulevard (Highway 71) between Interstate 35 and and Highway 183 to Lockhart. It is somewhat unique in the state park system, being a picnic and overnight camping park almost entirely surrounded by housing developments, and has been since its opening in 1976. This park features two scenic waterfalls along Onion Creek and was the ranch home of Thomas F. McKinney from 1850 until his death in 1873. The senior partner in McKinney and Williams, a commission house at the mouth of the Brazos in the 1830s, McKinney and Samuel May Williams used their credit with merchants in the United States to help supply the Texas army during the 1836 revolution against Santa Anna. Later McKinney and Williams joined Michel B. Menard in developing the new town of Galveston, where McKinney lived from 1837 to 1850.

This brief book includes the highlights of McKinney's adventuresome life, how and why he acquired the almost 40,000 acres surrounding the park in 1839, and how the huge tract was developed. His land included the Pilot Knob to the south and what became Bergstrom Air Force Base, soon to be Austin's new airport, to the east. An effort has been made to include information about others who lived on his property along Onion Creek, including McKinney's family, friends, employees, and slaves.

1.
THE PARK LAND BEFORE 1850

THE SOLID-ROCK FORD on Onion Creek in McKinney Falls State Park north of the landmark Pilot Knob attracted nomadic hunter-gatherers five thousand years ago, perhaps even earlier. Archeological evidence indicates the presence of ancient campsites in the rock shelters along the stream. A recent study of seventeenth- and eighteenth-century travel routes between San Antonio and Nacogdoches reveals that the Spanish followed the ancient Indian trails along the south side of Onion Creek to its mouth and a crossing on the Colorado River. Nineteenth-century Texas natives continued to use this path until the Anglo Texans dominated the area in the 1840s.[1]

The haunting ruins of Thomas Freeman McKinney's 1850s stone house overlook this ford and the scenic lower waterfall on Onion Creek. If the water in the creek is low, visitors can cross this volcanic outflow from the Pilot Knob and climb the hill to view the foundation and remaining walls of what was once a comfortable home. In 1974 before developing the park and opening it to the public, Texas Parks and Wildlife archeologists and members of the Texas Archaeological Society carefully excavated the homesite and other sites of interest. A few of the artifacts they found are displayed in the park's Smith Interpretive Center along with photographs of the McKinneys and exhibits explaining the unique geologic formations, the flora and fauna, and other material.

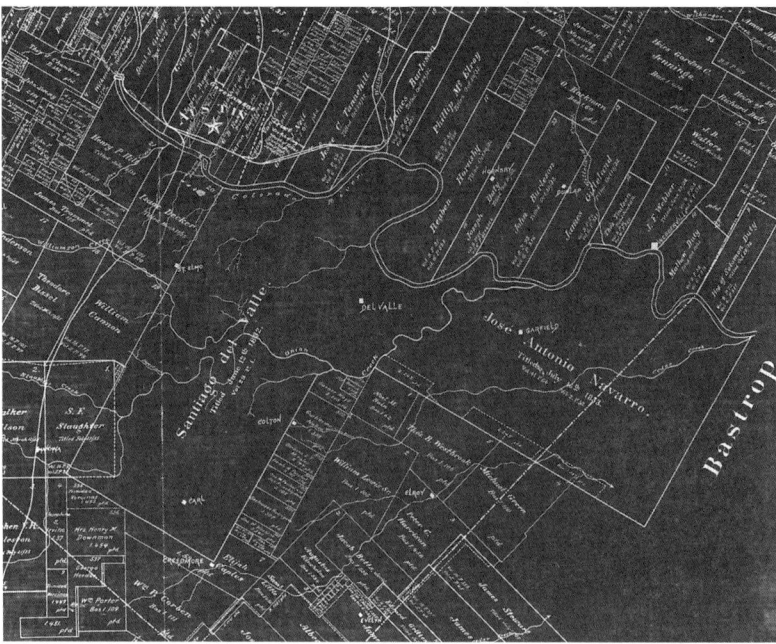

Thomas McKinney's land was part of the Santiago del Valle land grant south of the Colorado River. Detail from Travis County map, Texas General Land Office, 1894. *Courtesy Center for American History, University of Texas at Austin, CN 10122.*

The 672 acres that now make up the state park represent only a small portion of the undeveloped nine leagues (39,852 acres) that McKinney bought in the Santiago del Valle survey in 1839. While Del Valle was the the orignial patentee, he was a politician in the neighboring state of Coahuila and never even visited Texas. After Mexico won its independence from Spain, sparsely populated Texas and Coahuila were temporarily joined as a single state when the Mexican constitution was adopted in 1824. Hoping to increase the Hispanic presence in Texas and counter the growing Anglo Texan majority, Coahuila-Texas allowed native-born Mexicans to purchase unlocated eleven-league grants in Texas at low cost, expecting them to use the land to found new towns. Del Valle, however, like other Mexican speculators, defeated the government's intent by selling his unlocated Texas land grants to Anglo Texans.[2]

The history of the Del Valle tract illustrates Texas land speculating fever in the 1830s among both native Mexicans and Anglo American newcomers. Stephen F. Austin bought three unlocated grants from Mexican politicians for $1,000 while he was in the state capital at Saltillo in 1832. He sent the necessary papers to his lieutenant, Samuel May Williams, for Williams to locate the huge tracts and have them surveyed. Austin intended one for his personal use to be on the north side of the Colorado River near Mount Bonnell. Another was to be surveyed on the south bank along Onion Creek and in 1833 Austin told Williams to locate the Santiago del Valle grant (now only ten leagues and apparently Williams's property) on that site if Williams so desired. The ten leagues may represent Austin's payment for Williams's services, while the other league (4,428 acres) paid for a survey. Austin warned his assistant to complete the paperwork because the expiration date on locating these grants was approaching and added that similar unlocated permits were then selling for huge sums— up to $10,000 each—at the state capital.

Williams, as agent for Del Valle, had the Anglo Texan alcalde in San Felipe, the capital of Austin's colony, complete the transaction. Using the same power of attorney from Del Valle, Williams then sold the undeveloped ten leagues (44,280 acres) on the frontier to business associate Michel B. Menard for $2,500 (5.6 cents per acre) on July 16, 1835. Four years later on February 8, 1839, one month after the Republic of Texas Congress chose the land across the Colorado River for the new capital named Austin, McKinney, still in partnership with Williams, bought the Del Valle tract from Menard. McKinney paid $4,500 (11 cents an acre) for what was then a nine-league (39,852 acres) tract.[3] Seemingly its location across the river from the new capital city increased the property's value. All of these amounts except Austin's first $1,000 most likely were debts owed on other business ventures in a frontier society dependent on scarce gold coins, personal IOUs, heavily discounted paper money, and barter.

McKinney regarded his nine leagues on the western edge of the settlements as a future project and postponed developing his ranch on Onion Creek until almost 1850. Economic hard times during the Republic of Texas between 1836 and 1845 forced him to remain cautious. Also, the frontier was vulnerable to raids by both Indians and Mexicans. Although the town of Austin was established in 1839 and Travis County was created the following year, the area around the infant capital remained a sparsely settled frontier. In fact, the remote village was temporarily abandoned as the capital in 1842 and moved to Washington on the Brazos River when Mexican military raiders briefly occupied San Antonio in March and again in September. The frontier capital was reborn in July 1845 when delegates held a convention there to approve the annexation of Texas to the United States. Following annexation, Austin remained the state capital and McKinney began to make plans for Onion Creek.

2.
THOMAS F. MCKINNEY BEFORE MOVING TO ONION CREEK, 1801–1850

THOMAS FREEMAN MCKINNEY was born November 1, 1801, the eldest son of Abraham and Eleanor "Nelly" Prather McKinney. He had four sisters and three brothers. Neighbors recognized McKinney's father as a great hunter who took minimal interest in farming or raising horses like his father, Charles. Charles McKinney, an immigrant, arrived in Virginia in the 1750s and raised horses on the Virginia-North Carolina border in an area where neighbors raced thoroughbreds and quarter horses. In 1784 Charles moved his family and the horses through the Cumberland Gap into the Kentucky bluegrass region. Young "Freeman," as his mother called him in honor of her step-grandfather, adopted the skills of both his father and grandfather; he appreciated good horses and was an excellent marksman. Abraham moved his family west to Christian County, Kentucky, by 1811 and onward to Howard County, Missouri Territory, in 1819.[1]

In 1823 at age twenty-two, and now known as "Mac" to his friends, McKinney took his horse and rifle to follow the Santa Fe trail with his distant cousin Philip Allen Sublett, kin to the mountain men of that name. The cousins joined Stephen Cooper's second expedition to Santa Fe that left Franklin, Missouri, in May 1823, with pack horses loaded with trading goods. The party suffered a serious Indian attack southwest of Fort Osage and some members suffered terrible thirst when the group lost its way between water holes taking the Cimarron Cutoff in southwestern Kansas. They finally reached Santa Fe in November, where they discovered that the townspeople had already spent their money on the goods of a group of Missouri traders that had arrived earlier. The two adventurers joined an armed group heading south through El Paso to Chihuahua, which was a major trading outpost. Its residents were eager for United States-made goods, and unlike Santa Fe residents dependent on the arrival of annual payrolls, had a ready silver supply with a mint and a thriving economy. The cousins may have even travelled south to Durango.[2] During this journey, the pair learned sufficient Spanish for trading purposes.

McKinney was well suited to this lifestyle by temperament and training. In the 1870s his younger brother James P. McKinney described him thus: "He was about five feet ten inches tall, broad-shouldered, of muscular build, and weighed ordinarily about 170 pounds." He had a "fair common English education for the times, writing and spelling with grammatical correctness." Fond of adventure, he never knew fear, loved excitement and change, and generally remained firm, resolute, genial and warm hearted. Though a man of "strong prejudices" he was always just, liberal to a fault, and had both bitter enemies and many warm, ardent friends. However, his temper was quick and easily excited, "often unreasonably so," and his anger vehement. James added that his brother was a man of impulses who did things on the spur of the moment, often contrary to better judgment, but was usually hopeful and trusted that all things would come out right in the end.[3]

McKinney and Sublett decided not to retrace their steps, but to return home by way of Texas. Mac's uncle Stephen Prather, his mother's brother, lived near Nacogdoches where he had an Indian trading post on Attoyac Bayou, the present-day boundary between Nacogdoches and San Augustine counties. He traded with the nearby Alabama and Coushatta villages, exchanging merchandise for livestock, which he forwarded to Louisiana. McKinney and Sublett's route to Texas led through Saltillo, the capital of Coahuila-Texas, where they most likely bought horses and pack animals, which were in demand in Texas. The pair stopped in San Felipe, the center of Stephen F. Austin's colony on the Brazos River, where a number of Missouri and Kentucky residents were settling. McKinney applied for and received a headright league of land on August 16, 1824. This was the standard land grant of 4,428 acres to a head of a family at the low cost of $192 in fees paid to the surveyor, the clerk, and the state land commissioner. He located his league close to the San Antonio-Nacogdoches road crossing of the Brazos River not far from the present-day campus of Texas A&M University, and hoped it would be an excellent site for resting livestock or travelers along the major road.[4]

McKinney never developed the site, however, and instead he and Sublett settled in the Nacogdoches district and both were married by 1828. Mac and his wife, Nancy Watts, had a store and home on the square in the town of Nacogdoches and met Indian traders at a campground east of town. It was during this period that Mac met Michel B. Menard, a French Canadian trader who accompanied a band of Shawnee into eastern Texas. Menard had been their resident trader in Missouri and Arkansas while connected with his uncle Pierre Menard's trading house at Kaskaskia.[5]

About 1829 Mac acquired a slave who could handle horses and accompany him on his travels. Cary McKinney, as he was known when he gained his freedom, became an express rider during the Texas Revolution in 1836. This meant that Cary knew Texas geography well enough to take messages almost anywhere and avoid capture. In November 1839 Cary, with his petition for emancipation, took a wagon load of supplies from Galveston to Austin, the new capital of the Republic. The certificate Thomas McKinney signed said, "Bearer, a man of color," had been his slave for ten years and was faithful, honest, had carried messages besides earning the money to buy himself, his wife, and child. Sam Williams, a member of Congress, was already in the new town and was waiting for his trunk, which was on the wagon.[6]

McKinney seemed to have had a closer personal relationship with his few black bondsmen than did most slaveholders. He never was a planter or farmer who needed a large number of field hands. The most slaves he ever owned was twenty-one in 1860, which included seven under the age of ten; because they lived in five houses, small family groups appear to have been the norm. From the meager evidence in family letters and documents, it appears the McKinney blacks were house servants, horse handlers, and handymen who maintained the barns, the garden, planted oats, helped at the mill, and hauled water to the house overlooking Onion Creek. This was probably similar to the pattern of McKinney's father and grandfather. Abraham owned a maximum of nine slaves (three over age sixteen) between 1797 and 1817 according to tax records in Lincoln and Christian County, Kentucky. One family story mentioned a black majordomo who directed the Charles McKinney move through the Cumberland Gap. After Mac moved to Galveston in 1837, he helped Cary acquire town lots from the Galveston City Company and build the only livery stable in town. In 1846 Cary owned three lots, seven horses, and three carriages. He died soon after, but his wife and married daughter still lived there in 1850. One Galvestonian recalled that in 1838, Cary was the "best armed" among the twenty-seven men who rallied when the night sentry mistook a creaky oxcart for a Mexican invasion force.[7]

By the end of 1830, Mac and Nancy left East Texas and moved to San Felipe, where McKinney entered a partnership with Jared E. Groce, whose cotton plantation, Bernardo, was near present-day Hempstead. McKinney, Groce, & Company experimented in taking Groce's cotton to Saltillo in 1830 and 1831 because of the high nine-cents-a-pound tariff levied in New Orleans on imported Mexican (Texas) cotton that only brought the seller eighteen cents per pound. In December 1830 Mac traveled to Saltillo with twelve mules laden with cotton, but he found the route difficult because of a lack of grass and water. The next year he chartered a schooner and took the cotton to Matamoros, where he hired carts to take the bales to Saltillo. That, too, proved expensive because the Saltillo mill was not in operation and he had to continue south to San Luis Potosi. On the return from that city, bandits attacked McKinney's silver-laden mule train. Mac's mule drivers cut loose the bags in case the animals stampeded and fired at the robbers killing three and wounding others. McKinney's skill with his rifle impressed the countryside, and the governor arrested the thieves, whose leader had been McKinney's host the previous evening. Mac's only loss was one mule.[8]

The brief association with Groce was only one of McKinney's business ventures at this time. He helped Michel B. Menard build a sawmill on the lower Trinity River and gradually increased his land holdings by taking acreage to settle debts. At the end of 1833 McKinney forged a new partnership with Samuel May Williams to open a commission house at the mouth of the Brazos River. Mac was to handle the the physical side of buying and selling livestock and agricultural products while Williams was to keep the books and use his family's extensive mercantile connections in the United States for credit and contacts. Stephen F. Austin gave them land on the west side of the river near the mouth for a townsite they named Quintana, probably for a commercial associate in San Luis Potosi. During 1834 McKinney erected a warehouse and store and built homes for himself and Williams; he soon added a wharf, a boatways, and a cotton gin.[9]

Trouble with the Mexican customs collector and troops stationed opposite Quintana at Velasco and at Anahuac on upper Galveston Bay took place while McKinney was absent in June 1832. The Anglo Texans forced the administration troops to withdraw and claimed that they were acting in concert with General Santa Anna, then a federalist reformer, who had led the successful civil war against the centralist administration.

In January 1835 the customs collectors and troops returned to Texas ports and in May a patrol boat seized and confiscated McKinney's new schooner, *Columbia*, as it arrived at the Brazos from New Orleans. He was on board and the cruiser's captain accused him of smuggling and having passengers without passports. McKinney and the passengers were released, but the cargo retained. This incident and a similar seizure in Galveston Bay angered Anglo Texans sufficiently to resist President Santa Anna's resumption of the despised tariff policy. With the aid of his New Orleans trading partners, McKinney acquired another schooner, the *San Felipe*, which he ordered armed before it left the Crescent City in July with Mexican patriot Lorenzo de Zavala. An opponent of Santa Anna and now a refugee, Zavala came to Texas to arouse resistance to the administration. Zavala stayed with the McKinneys at Quintana and Mac introduced him to political leaders at San Felipe, Brazoria, and Columbia.[10]

The armed *San Felipe* brought Stephen F. Austin to Quintana from New Orleans on September 1, 1835. Austin had left Texas in April 1833 carrying petitions to Mexico City for reforms, including separate statehood for Texas. A hasty letter Austin wrote during a fit of despondency ended up in the hands of the authorities who considered it seditious and reason enough to arrest Austin and hold him until mid-1835. As the *San Felipe* approached the Brazos, the captain saw the *Correo Mexicana* about to seize the U.S. brig *Tremont* as it unloaded lumber at McKinney's wharf. Sending Austin and other passengers ashore, the captain prepared to attack, but adverse wind prevented immediate pursuit. McKinney and volunteers with rifles boarded McKinney's new steamboat *Laura*, which was already in the river, and headed into the Gulf to tow the *San Felipe* into firing position. The action could be seen from shore and the schooner's cannon forced the the *Correo* to surrender. The Texans sent the officers and crew of the *Correo* to New Orleans to be tried as pirates in the U. S. District Court.[11]

During the ensuing struggle for independence from Mexico, Williams went to the United States to negotiate loans for the new Republic of Texas while McKinney used the firm's credit in New Orleans and Mobile to obtain supplies for the Texas volunteer army. When word reached the Brazos about the fall of the Alamo in mid-March, families began moving east and McKinney took responsiblity for Sarah Williams and her three boys; and the families of James W. Fannin, in command at Goliad; and William H. Jack, who was with Sam Houston's army. Minerva Fort Fannin and daughter Pinckney had just arrived in Texas and lived with McKinney while Laura Harrison Jack and her three children resided across the Brazos River above Velasco. The McKinneys and the Jacks had been close friends since 1830 when they all lived in San Felipe; Mac was godfather to Thomas McKinney Jack, the

Thomas F. McKinney by unknown photographer, c. 1850. Daguerreotype, 3 x 2¹/₂ inches. *Courtesy Texas State Library and Archives Commission.*

Anna Gray Gibbs McKinney, c. 1864. *Photograph courtesy Texas State Library and Archives Commission.*

eldest child. Without children of his own, Mac took a keen interest in the Williams, Jack, and Fannin children. The McKinneys and their friends boarded the steamboat *Laura* for Sabine Pass and the new town of Georgia that Mac had founded near the mouth of the Neches River (present-day Port Neches). Mac left the women and children there and took his steamboat to New Orleans for supplies. The women remained there until July when Mac brought them home on board the steamboat *Yellowstone*. McKinney helped settle the Fannin estate, and following the death of Mrs. Fannin about 1838, became the guardian of her two daughters. The second, Minerva, born at the Jack residence in late 1836, was mentally retarded—some said as a result of Mrs. Fannin's visit to Santa Anna while he was held prisoner at a nearby plantation during her pregnancy.[12]

In 1833 McKinney and Williams had become partners with Michel B. Menard in a complicated scheme to acquire a Mexican title to one league of land on the eastern tip of Galveston Island. For reasons of national security neither Spain nor Mexico had permitted anyone to live on the island, which had the best natural harbor on the Texas Gulf coast. In 1836 Menard had to take in additional partners in order to secure sufficient funds to win approval from the First Congress of the Republic of Texas for his Mexican title and to establish the Galveston City Company. Sometime between 1837 and 1838 the firm of McKinney and Williams closed their business at Quintana and moved to the new town of Galveston, locating their warehouses and wharf on the Strand at Twenty-third Street.[13]

The 1837 banking panic in the United States resulted in the failure of many banks and commission houses; the resulting downward spiral of the economy lasted for almost a decade and seriously affected Texas. This lack of circulating coins at a time when paper money was not recognized legal tender caused the firm of McKinney and Williams to issue its own paper money to aid local commerce. Business worries kept Williams in the United States while McKinney struggled in Galveston. The pair finally sold their interest in the commission house to Williams's brother Henry in 1841 in order to end their indebtedness to him. Williams continued his efforts to establish a bank at Galveston while Mac monitored his extensive land holdings and other investments. The former partners continued to serve on the Board of Directors of the Galveston City Company under its president, M. B. Menard.[14]

Meanwhile, the McKinney marriage was deteriorating. Mac was often away from the island and, according to friends, was seemingly irritable about business matters and personal relationships. Sarah Williams was living with the McKinneys on the island in October 1838 and she and Mac quarrelled about where her children should go to school, leaving her so upset that she left to live with her widowed mother who had a home along the San Jacinto estuary. The previous year a visitor at the McKinney home described Nancy as "a tolerably good looking woman, but pale, with falling features, looking unhappy." By early 1840 Nancy resided with the Jacks at Velasco while Mac lived with his good friend Dr. Levi Jones and his wife in Galveston. Lucy Jones maintained a lively correspondence with Laura Jack (and always inquired about Nancy) because the Jack children lived with the Joneses in order to attend school in Galveston.[15]

Exactly when McKinney fell in love with Anna Gibbs is unknown. The eldest of the three daughters of Mary Ellen Gibbs, a widowed Boston schoolteacher, Anna was twenty years old in 1838 when she and her mother opened a school in Galveston. Mrs. Gibbs came to the island at the suggestion of Sam Williams's brother in Mobile, who considered her a good teacher. Anna was a vigorous athletically inclined young woman who loved horseback riding, and McKinney had several horses at his residence on the west end of town. He built his home and that of Williams between 1838 and 1839 on ten-acre outlots as did many other business leaders. He also had laid off a racecourse nearby as an enticement for the Galveston City Company.[16]

Anna and Mac's deepening friendship probably caused Nancy McKinney to leave the island. After she left, Mac sold a quarter of the block where his home was to Anna's sister Caroline in September 1840, and his home near the corner of Forty-first Street and Avenue Q to Anna and her mother. Caroline and Mrs. Gibbs went to Boston to visit in the summer of 1841, and McKinney, who was in Baltimore on business with Henry Howell Williams, joined them on board the steamboat *New York* in October for the return to Galveston. Anna and Mac's relationship grew and in 1842, at age forty-one, Mac caused a scandal by divorcing Nancy and marrying Anna. The only means for a divorce was to petition the Congress of the Republic for approval and then appear before a district court judge. Mac submitted his application to Congress during its special sesssion at Houston in May 1842, and after it passed the House, Senator William H. Jack moved to approve the petition, which was done. The document was signed by Mac's friend, President Sam Houston. The Galveston District Court heard the case titled Nancy McKinney v. T. F. McKinney on September 7, 1842, and granted the divorce on the grounds of mutual abandonment for more than two years and an amicable division of property. Anna and Mac married in Galveston on September 23, 1842. Like Nancy, Anna did not have any children.[17]

McKinney had always owned horses that could participate in the local races but by 1839, at least, he invested in thoroughbreds. By that time Mac owned Osceola, then five years old, whose pedigree went back to the famous Sir Archy in Viriginia. McKinney admired that stud so much that he acquired a painting of Sir Archy, which hung above the mantel of his home both on the island and later on Onion Creek. Osceola ran in the April 1839 races at the New Market Course at Velasco along with Mac's other thoroughbred, Tom Thurman. Both were listed in *The American Stud Book*. The track at Velasco faded away and unfortunately no records have been discovered for McKinney's track at Galveston. The circular mile-and-a-half sand track was between Thirty-seventh and Forty-fifth Avenues south of R Street near the Gulf. Perhaps the high water during a storm in 1842 washed away the rail fence that enclosed the racecourse where Francis C. Sheridan, grandson of the English playwright, bet on a horse named Boston in early 1840.[18]

Sheridan, on a diplomatic assignment, was impressed by McKinney's attire and demeanor when the Englishman boarded the steamboat *Constitution* at Velasco for the trip to Galveston. Mac was wearing a "frock coat made out of a scarlet blanket with

Thomas and Anna McKinney, left, and Ada Bradley at the Onion Creek Ranch, c. 1863. *Photograph courtesy Texas State Library and Archives Commission.*

a black edging" and the writer was surprised to find another gentlemen wearing an identical one in green. Canadian style coats were evidently popular in Galveston, but it was McKinney's picking his teeth with a Bowie knife that delighted Sheridan, who did not understand that Texans knew how to entertain visitors.[19]

After Texas was annexed to the United States, voters in Galveston chose McKinney as their state senator to attend the First Legislature, which opened in Austin on February 16, 1846. There McKinney witnessed the symbolic lowering of the Lone Star flag and the raising of the Stars and Stripes three days later. Little was accomplished during the first session because the war with Mexico began in May. Mac used the trip to Austin to make plans for his ranch on Onion Creek.[20]

United States troops moved south toward the Rio Grande and many of Mac's friends and his nephew left the island to join in the war. One friend was Albert Sidney Johnston, a graduate of the United States Military Academy at West Point, who had come to

Texas after the Battle of San Jacinto and in August 1836 was named general of the Texas army. In 1838 Johnston served in the cabinet of President Mirabeau B. Lamar and invested in a Brazos River plantation. During Johnston's absences from Texas in the 1840s, Mac served as one of his agents. In May 1846, Johnston became Colonel of the First Texas Rifle Volunteers, and Eliza Johnston and the wives of other officers remained in Galveston with friends. Mac and Anna invited a lively group to visit their home close to the beach. The young women rode the McKinney horses on the beach by moonlight, spent the night, and enjoyed playing the piano with Pinckney Fannin, who lived with the McKinneys as did her sister Minerva. Another delight was "sea bathing" to cool off during the hot summer. Major Philip N. Barbour, also a West Pointer from Kentucky like the Johnstons, forbade his pretty young wife to go into the water, but Eliza Johnston coaxed her and soon the group, dressed in shortened skirts, held hands and waded knee-deep into the waves. When Martha Barbour became confident enough to let the waves splash over her, she went to town and bought a rubberized bathing cap like the others wore. Martha Hopkins Barbour was the grand-daughter of Samuel Hopkins, aide to George Washington; she stayed with her uncle, District Court Judge James Love, in Galveston.[21]

Thus, four years after their marriage, Galveston society was comfortable with Mac and Anna and the scandal receded. Soon, however, the McKinneys abandoned the easy pleasant lifestyle of Galveston Island for Onion Creek in Travis County. Instead of wading in the gulf, venturesome Anna could enjoy the rushing water of the creek and the upper and lower waterfalls and hunt coyotes while riding around the hills. Gregarious people, the McKinneys always welcomed a steady stream of visitors to their hill country ranch just as they had in Galveston.

3.
MCKINNEY FALLS RANCH, 1847–1859: A GROWING FAMILY COMPOUND

THE RANCH BEGAN IN 1847 when Mac's brother, James Prather McKinney, moved his family from Galveston to Onion Creek. James was eighteen years younger than Mac, the next to youngest of the nine living children of Abraham and Nelly. In 1837 at age eighteen James had joined McKinney and Williams at Quintana as a junior clerk and the following year married his cousin Elvira, the daughter of Stephen Prather. Elvira was the same age as James and the young couple remained in Quintana to close the business through mid-1839, when their first child was born. They then moved to Galveston, where James continued to work for firm until it was sold to Henry Williams. Between 1842 and 1847, James helped tend to his brother's scattered property, collecting rents, payments, and running off squatters or timber thieves. The couple had three children when they settled in their home along Williamson Creek, a lesser stream that emptied into Onion Creek near the upper falls.[1]

Mac transferred $9,000 in slaves and livestock to James as payment for his past services with McKinney and Williams. Five adult blacks and four children accompanied the caravan to Travis County and helped the herders drive the three stallions, seven mares, three hundred head of cattle, and seven hundred sheep and goats that Mac had kept pastured in Fort Bend and other mainland counties along the way. Mac had begun breeding imported sheep in Fort Bend County in 1840—Bakewells from England, Merinos from Vermont, and a cross of Merinos and Southdowns from Ohio. He crossed them with Mexican stock, but they did not thrive in the humid weather. He correctly surmised that the sheep would do better on the Onion Creek property. By 1850, James had 60 acres under cultivation and owned 1,400 hundred more acres in the tract where he kept 40 horses, 15 mules, 14 oxen, and grazed 80 cattle and 125 sheep.[2]

Mac had problems with creditors, and in 1848 he placed the remaining 3,800 acres in his Del Valle tract in Anna's name to protect it. Texas community property laws, adapted from Mexican law, not only gave wives one-half of the property acquired during marriage, but also allowed married women to hold property in their own names, a privilege not available in most states at that time. In 1848, the Travis County tax assessor valued absentee-owner Anna's Onion Creek acreage at $8,220, including three slaves, four horses, 170 head of cattle, and one wagon. James managed the entire property. James's property that year was assessed at $8,603 for 2,158 acres, slaves, and livestock.[3]

Galvestonians again sent McKinney to the Second and Third Legislatures (1847–1850) but as a member of the House of Representatives, where he served on the finance committee, an assignment he no doubt solicited. Texas had retained its public lands and its public debt when it was annexed in 1845, but the new state lacked the means to pay debts stemming from the Republic, including the large sum owed the firm of McKinney and Williams. After a public referendum in November 1850, the state agreed to accept $10 million from the United States in exchange for a somewhat nebulous claim to New Mexico's territory east of the Rio Grande. This surrender created the modern boundary of Texas and also provided funds to pay off many of Texas's creditors stemming from the Revolution. McKinney, of course, hoped that he could at long last recover the $99,000 owed to McKinney and Williams for expenditures made during the struggle against Santa Anna. Six years later, in 1856, the legislators appropriated a scaled-back amount of $40,729 for the firm, but as McKinney explained to his former partner, they each received only $8,000—

the rest was for "loans" to those who helped pass the measure.[4]

During these years Mac remained a resident of Galveston and was involved in a number of business activities when not attending the legislature. He made several trips to New Orleans according to the passenger lists published in the Galveston *Weekly News* and scattered references in the correspondence of his former partner. He acquired Menard's interest in their sawmill on the Trinity River and shipped lumber to a Houston merchant. McKinney, Williams, and Menard were members of a Galveston committee in December 1848 that planned the Galveston-Brazos Canal, a private venture that was under way in 1850, but numerous bank cave-ins hampered its success. Both Brazos River planters and Galveston merchants hoped a canal parallel to the Gulf from the river through the marshes and Galveston's West Bay would provide safer passage for cotton shipments; the treacherous sandbars at the mouth of the Brazos caused many vessels to go aground and wreck, which resulted in high insurance rates. McKinney had also contracted with Galveston County's commissioners court in 1846 to build a private wagon bridge from Teichman's Point on the island to Virginia Point on the mainland (the present causeway); financial difficulties prevented construction but he retained the privilege through 1866. By that time, however, a railroad bridge had been completed at that site in 1859, which lessened the need for a wagon bridge.[5]

Between 1850 and 1852, McKinney built his stone house and a gristmill on Onion Creek just below the homesite. Ox teams hauled heavy cypress and cedar timbers from a stand of trees on Sam Williams's land in Bastrop County. The mill, intended to produce income, was a priority. Mac created a dam for a millpond and a diversionary canal through the step-down limestone ledge and the outflow lava rock from the ancient eruption from the Pilot Knob. This unusual deposit lined the stream bed near the lower falls. Inside the wheelhouse, the water turned a four-foot in diameter metal-and-wood horizontal turbine that provided the power to turn the grindstones; the water returned to the creek by a tailrace beneath the mill. The Austin *Texas State Gazette* noted on July 10, 1852, that "the Honorable Thomas F. McKinney has erected an

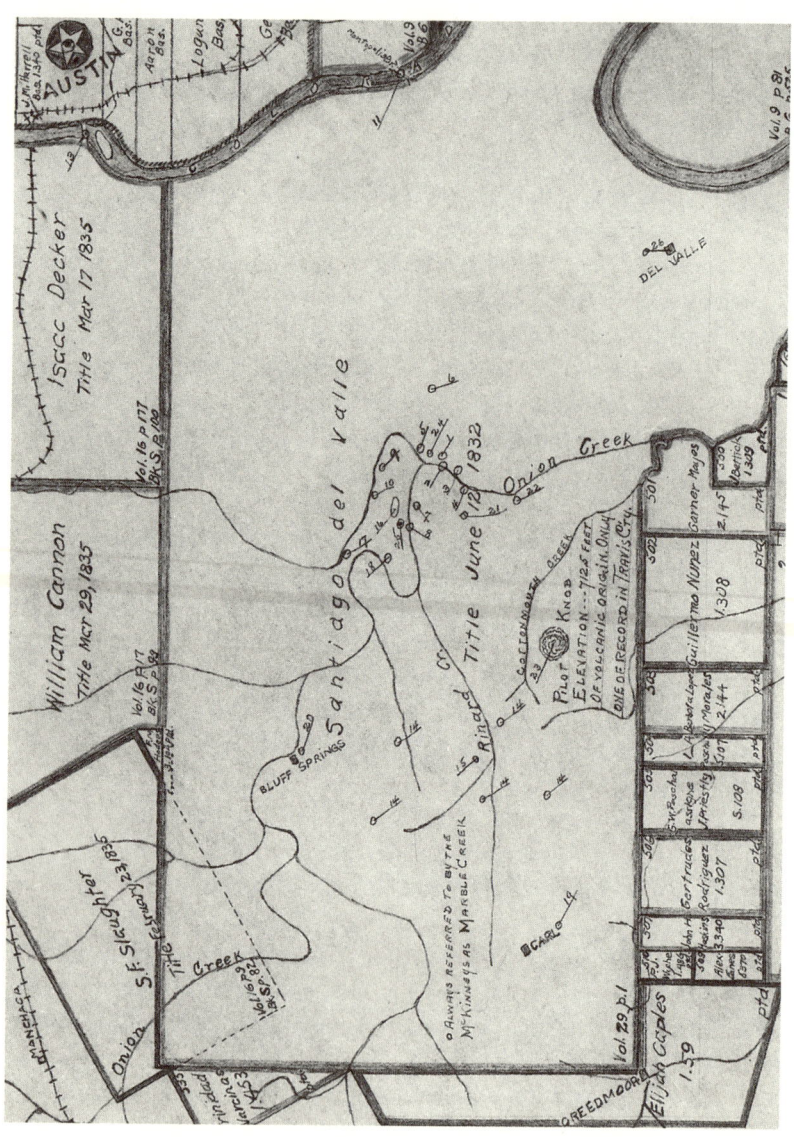

Descriptions of the numbered areas on the map are based on handwritten notes by Reynolds K. Lowry, c. 1940. The area shown is a detail from a larger map.

1. Thomas F. and Anna G. McKinney home at McKinney Falls on Onion Creek, eight miles south of Austin.
2. McKinney Falls at McKinneys' home about 300 feet south of the house and about 250 feet below where Williamson Creek flows into Onion Creek.
3. Remains of the old mill on the north bank of Onion and not more than 250 feet from the falls. The mill was destroyed by a flood in 1869.
4. House occupied by R. W. Lowry when he first came to the McKinney home from Virginia in 1872. This building was not more than 350 feet from the horse trainer's cabin.
5. Slave graveyard on the east bank of Williamson Creek near the mouth of Williamson Creek where it empties into Onion Creek.
6. A large tenant house where the McKinney slaves lived.
7. Horse trainer's home—a large two-room stone dwelling with a six-foot fireplace in the south room.
8. Upper falls on Onion Creek.
9. "Bob Field," a tract farmed by a black man named Bob Holman.
10. The jenny pasture lay west and south of Bob Field.
11. Site of Montopolis Bridge.
12. Winter ground of McKinney thoroughbreds (not shown on this detail).
13. Site of Colorado River bridge.
14. Area (see x's on map) where Thomas and Anna McKinney rode for pleasure and hunted wolves and coyotes.
15. Rinard Creek is a tributary of Onion Creek entirely situated within the Santiago del Valle grant. The McKinneys referred to it as Marble Creek.
16. The McKinneys' private racetrack on the bank of Onion Creek half a mile from horse trainer John Van Hagen's cabin.
17. Home (two log cabins) of McKinney servant Lazaro Garza.
18. Temporary home of Dr. Josephus Steiner before he married and moved to the west bank of Onion Creek.
19. Carl, Texas, a small settlement.
20. Bluff Springs on the east bank of Onion Creek.
21. The site of the red circular lime kiln on the west bank of Onion Creek below McKinney Falls.
22. Buzzard Roost. No connection to the McKinneys.
23. Pilot Knob, the remains of an extinct volcano.
24. The large two-story horse barn for the thoroughbreds about 250 feet west of the big house and near where Williamson Creek flows into Onion.
25. Not included in Reynolds Lowry notes.
26. Del Valle, Texas, established mid-1870s.

Map and notes courtesy the Texas State Library and Archives Commission.

elegant flouring mill on Onion Creek four miles from the city and is prepared to manufacture flour of superior quality." Local farmers were experimenting with various strains of wheat in hopes of avoiding high-priced imported flour. The mill, which could grind all sorts of grain, operated until a flood in 1869 destroyed the machinery.[6] The flood waters along the creek did not reach the McKinney residence or the large barn for the thoroughbreds on the hill.

Details about the building of Mac's house are lacking and information relies on archaeological investigations conducted in 1974. The house was built with soft native limestone quarried downstream along Onion Creek; the blocks were cut with a circular saw and then shaped to size with chisel and ax. The floor joists, beams, rafters, and flooring were cypress or cedar, as were the door and window frames and the shakes for the roof. Six square pillars extended from the ground to support the second-story porch roof. The interior walls and ceilings were plastered and the fireplaces were of uncut limestone.

The house was a one-room-deep rectangle (approximately forty by twenty feet) with three rooms on each floor accessed from a ten-foot-wide covered porch both upstairs and down. The galleries also served as outdoor living space in pleasant weather. A wide stairway parallel with and attached to the south exterior wall began just east of the center door on the first floor. Each room had a door to the porch and the center room also had a window on the gallery. Windows on the north and east provided cross ventilation, but the west wall appears to have had no openings. The west rooms were about seventeen feet square, the center rooms about twelve by seventeen, and the east rooms about nine by seventeen. A double fireplace formed a portion of the stone wall dividing the center and east rooms and the two had a connecting inside door perpendicular to the north wall. The fireplaces and the door were repeated on the second floor.[7]

The McKinneys had lived comfortably in Galveston and doubtless brought their wood cooking stove and Anna's piano to their new home. The oil painting of Sir Archy, the Virginia thoroughbred, hung on the wall and when there was company Anna used

The cabin of John Van Hagen, Thomas McKinney's horse trainer, 1943. *Photograph by Reynolds K. Lowry, courtesy Texas State Library and Archives Commission.*

china and silver she had inherited from her family. Wardrobes, bureaus, and trunks held the best clothing, including a yellow silk ball gown Mac brought Anna from New Orleans. According to family lore, she wore the gown to Gov. E. M. Pease's inaugural ball and danced with Sam Houston.[8]

The five slave houses that the 1860 census enumerator listed were probably on the north side of the house. An annotated 1940s map by Mac's great-grandnephew, Reynolds Lowry, who was born in the house in 1876, shows an oblong perpendicular to the residence in the forty-acre field labeled "commodious tenant house for negroes." A two-story horse barn for the thoroughbreds lay along the ridge overlooking the mouth of Williamson Creek about 250 feet west of the McKinney residence. On the south side of the house toward the creek were two sixteen-feet-deep stone cisterns lined with mortar; the remains of metal pipes indicate that rainwater from the roof was funneled into the cisterns.[9] No evidence of a well or pump suggests that bathing and clothes washing, especially during dry spells, probably took place in the creek.

While the pampered thoroughbreds had their barn and special pastures, the ordinary breeding stock was confined within stacked stone fences, one as high as five feet, on the south side of Onion

Creek. A portion of a corral, about eighty by two hundred and sixty feet, remains near the south boundary of the park. The small stone house where horse trainer John Van Hagen lived was in that area too. Van Hagen worked McKinney's horses from about 1852 until the early 1870s. His snug house, about twenty-nine by seventeen feet of mortared stone blocks, had a cedar-shingled roof and a stone fireplace. It might have been used by the McKinneys or Enoch Martin, a longtime friend and stockhand, as a temporary residence in the early days.

Across Onion Creek in a flat area between it and Williamson Creek was the McKinney training track, where some races took place as late as the Civil War. Nearby was a fenced pasture for the McKinney mules while the rich grassland near the mouth of Onion Creek served as a winter pasture for the thoroughbreds. Mac also provided land for the Travis County Racing Association's track near the Colorado River southeast of the Montopolis bridge. Mac was president of the racing organization in the 1850s. The land west and south of the stone corrals and around the Pilot Knob was open range where the McKinneys and their friends rode horseback while hunting coyotes along Cottonmouth and Rinard (later Marble) creeks.[10]

In 1852 the McKinneys resumed caring for Minerva Fannin when those who were keeping her could no longer cope with the strong sixteen-year-old impaired young woman. Pinckney Fannin, her beautiful and well-educated sister, had died in Galveston in 1847. One of the McKinney slaves was assigned to watch Minerva until she was accepted at the new Austin Lunatic Asylum in 1861, where she remained until her death in either 1893 or 1897.[11]

McKinney served as one of the four Travis County commissioners from 1852 to 1856 and James followed him from 1857 to 1860 to represent Precinct Four. One of the main tasks was surveying and improving local roads. Property owners had to furnish labor for the improvements. Travis County Democrats elected McKinney to the Seventh Legislature, which opened in November 1857. The session was lively and unsettling with talk of secession. United States Senator Sam Houston had alienated many Texas Democrats in 1854 when he voted against the Kansas-Nebraska Act, which

Eleanor Prather McKinney, mother of Thomas F. McKinney, c. 1864. *Photograph courtesy Margaret Swett Henson.*

permitted slavery to expand north and west of Missouri contrary to the 1820 Missouri Compromise. As a lame duck senator, Houston ran for Texas governor in 1857 and was defeated. Mac, an ardent Democrat, still supported his old friend, who won the governor's race in 1859.[12]

The increasing tension in Missouri and Kansas over the slavery issue caused McKinney to urge his mother and siblings to leave Missouri and move to Onion Creek. His sister Euphemia, her husband James Walker Austin, and their seven children arrived by wagon train in October 1857. Austin built his home on 250 acres in the Del Valle tract just east of present State Highway 281 and south of the Bergstrom Air Force Base, which in the late 1990s became Austin's new airport. The following spring, Mac went to Missouri and brought his mother and the family of his brother Charles to Texas. Seventy-seven-year-old Eleanor Prather McKinney not only survived the jolting two-month journey by wagon, but lived seven more years until her death in 1865. In 1859 Eleanor McKinney's seventy-five-year-old sister, Elizabeth Prather Givens, joined the families on Onion Creek. Her son, Capt. Newton Curd Givens, a graduate of West Point and a veteran of the Mexican War, was ill with tuberculosis in San Antonio, where he died in March 1859. Givens's childless widow soon married M. T. Johnson and moved to Fort Worth. The McKinney ranch family compound increased again when the widow of Mac's cousin Thomas Prather, son of Stephen, arrived from San Augustine with her children. Except for the two elderly women, each family acquired a small tract and had its own home.[13]

Although content with his family nearby, the increasing talk about secession disturbed McKinney. Like his friend Sam Houston, McKinney was a unionist in sentiment, but state loyalty and economic survival forced him to make difficult decisions after Abraham Lincoln was elected president in 1860.

4.
THE MCKINNEYS: WARTIME AND THE AFTERMATH, 1860–1896

THE 1860 CENSUS reveals how much the McKinney brothers had improved their property on Onion Creek during the preceding decade. Mac had 1,500 improved acres with fences and structures valued at $48,000 and estimated his farm machinery, including the mill, to be worth an additional $10,500. He owned about 100 horses, 120 mules, 70 milch cows, 20 oxen, 250 range cattle, 15 hogs, and 900 sheep, for a total value of $36,000. During the past year Mac had harvested about 500 bushels of corn and 180 bushels of oats while the sheared sheep furnished 3,100 pounds of wool. From the cows' milk, he processed an estimated 500 pounds of butter. By these figures, the McKinney ranch was worth $95,000.

Mac did not raise cotton but James McKinney ginned eleven bales from a portion of his cultivated 130 acres. He also grew corn, Irish and sweet potatoes, and other vegetables in his "market garden." James had fewer animals with only fourteen horses, three mules, and fifty milk cows, but about the same number of oxen, range cattle, and hogs as his brother. James's property was a self-supporting farm rather than a breeding ranch like Mac's. The younger brother valued his land at $11,000, farm tools at $1,000, and his livestock at $4,500. Neither man owned many slaves: Mac had twenty-one including one couple both age seventy and a number of children housed in five dwellings while James had fifteen including one woman age fifty and youngsters under age ten living in a like number of structures. These blacks, while not free, were more like "family," who helped with housekeeping, child raising, planting, harvesting, and animal care, not gang labor under an overseer. There was a "slave" cemetery on the high bank on the north side of Onion Creek in a pecan grove just west of the McKinney house according to Reynolds Lowry, who grew up in the McKinney house in the 1870s. A descendant of one of these black families recalled oral history that his great-grandfather had come to Travis County as "slave companion of" James P. McKinney and after emancipation had bought seventy-three acres near the Pilot Knob. Although some of the details are in error, such as "John" for "James" and coming from Kentucky instead of Missouri, the story is convincing, especially when hints of close personal relationships are found in correspondence. For example, James wrote to Walker Austin from Quintana in 1838 and enclosed five cents for James's slave George who was with the Austins in Missouri; George was to spend the money on "anything he likes."[1]

The stone house was full when the census enumerator visited the McKinneys in July 1860. Besides Mac and Anna, his elderly mother, Eleanor Prather McKinney, and her sister, Elizabeth P. Givens, were there along with Minerva Fannin, age twenty-six. Horse trainer John Van Hagen also was listed, though perhaps he only took meals with the family. Nearby was the residence of Dr. Josephus Murray Steiner, one of Mac's good friends; Steiner became the superintendent of the new state "lunatic asylum" when it opened in May 1861 in Austin and served until 1865. Minerva Fannin was one of the first inmates in the new building.[2]

Mac met Steiner through his cousin Newton Curd Givens when Steiner was in Austin on trial for murder. Steiner had joined the army directly after medical school in Pennsylvania and came to Texas in 1847 during the Mexican War. Afterward he served at Fort Graham west of Fort Worth where he discovered that Maj. Ripley A. Arnold, the commanding officer on and off since 1851, was procuring U.S. government horses under questionable circumstances and selling them for his own profit. Steiner told

Arnold he intended to expose the scam and during an exchange of shots on September 6, 1853, Arnold died. A court martial assembled in Austin on April 15, 1854, but Steiner avoided arrest and surrendered himself to civil authorities in May. Steiner, represented in court by future governor Richard Coke and future Confederate general William H. Parsons, was acquitted. The military also closed the case but dropped Steiner from army rolls in May 1856. That same year Steiner married his sweetheart, Laura Fisher, in Ohio and brought her to Onion Creek where Mac sold him 240 acres not far from James McKinney's residence. Steiner sold the place in 1861 when he became superintendent at the asylum. Active in politics, Steiner had enemies. In 1866 the doctor received a death threat—details are lacking—and Mac hid the Steiners and their children until he could arrange for them to leave Texas. Laura Steiner returned to Austin with her children after the doctor's death in 1879 and resumed her friendship with Anna McKinney, who was also a widow by that time. Laura's son became the state health officer in 1911 while her daughter Adele is best remembered as the wife of Albert Sidney Burleson of Austin, who served as postmaster general in President Woodrow Wilson's cabinet.[3]

McKinney grew increasingly uneasy as the November 6, 1860, election approached with its four regional candidates: Republican Abraham Lincoln and Democrat Stephen A. Douglas, both northerners, and the Constitutional Union party's John Bell and Democrat John C. Breckinridge, both southerners. On November 22, still waiting for the results, the opinionated Mac lectured to Guy M. Bryan, nephew of Stephen F. Austin, who was the same age as James McKinney. Mac disapproved of Bryan's recent politics. A state legislator in the 1850s, Bryan had led Texas Democrats out of the regular party that had nominated Douglas but was now a leader in the new secession movement. Mac, who had supported Breckenridge, wrote that "the people of the North have a constitutional right to elect Mr. Lincoln" just as we have the right to choose Breckinridge. Mac, however, deplored Austinites who said that if Breckinridge won "we will fight to sustain the constitution" but in the same breath said if Lincoln won, "we will fight to violate the constitution." McKinney believed this was "utterly wrong."[4] In spite of philosophical and political differences with Bryan, the pair remained friends in part because Guy had married Laura Jack, the youngest daughter of Mac's late friend William H. Jack.

When word about Lincoln's election reached Austin, unionists like McKinney pleaded for calm and reason. Governor Houston refused to call the legislature to act on secession amid demands for a special convention to do so. Houston finally bowed to majority opinion and called a special session to meet in January, with any action taken to be subject to the voters' approval. The legislators met and immediately ordered a secession convention: those delegates convened January 28, 1861, and voted 152 to 6 to leave the union. Governor Houston called for a statewide referendum on secession for February 23, and to his chagrin, voters endorsed severing the ties by a vote of 46,153 to 14,747. However, more than one-half of the voters in Travis County cast ballots against secession. When the convention demanded that all current state officials take an oath of loyalty to the Confederate States of America on March 15, Governor Houston refused. The delegates declared the governor's office vacant and elevated Lieutenant Governor Edward Clark to the higher office.[5]

Some Austin unionists fled the area but McKinney remained. He and his kinsmen with unionist sentiments realistically chose loyalty to Texas over political differences. Economics dictated that they support the Confederacy by growing cotton to ship to Mexico, but they like most Texans complained about the ever-increasing taxes and the depreciation of Confederate money.[6]

The former Santa Fe trader did not volunteer to take cotton to the Rio Grande, not even in the huge broad-wheeled Chihuahua wagons used south of San Antonio. No doubt Confederate officials there sought his advice when he and Anna visited Sam Maverick and his wife in the Alamo City. McKinney joined two others in Austin in forming a trading company, Raymond, McKinney, and Furman, which gathered, baled, and bagged local cotton.[7]

The problem for merchants like McKinney was not only the difficult trip to Laredo, Eagle Pass, or the lower Rio Grande towns, but also the corruption and avarice on both sides of the river. Mexican merchants, customs officials, and even higher ranking officials took advantage of the Texan need to sell cotton and acquire goods. It was just as bad on the Texas side of the river where rival merchants and speculators competed with Confederate military commanders and government agents as well as state agents who were all trying to secure an advantage for their agencies and sometimes for themselves. Both the Confederate government and Texas officials tried to regulate the flow of cotton to Mexico by confiscating a portion of the planter's crop and giving government bonds in return—paper nobody trusted.[8]

In January 1864 Gen. E. Kirby Smith, commander of the Confederate Trans-Mississippi Department at Shreveport, called McKinney and Judge Thomas J. Devine of San Antonio into service to negotiate a settlement of a recent Mexican seizure of Confederate assets on the border. The year before, the Confederate quartermaster at San Antonio had discovered that the commander of the fort at Brownsville had confiscated a shipment of Confederate cotton to pay debts belonging to his command. The irate Mexican merchant involved in the shipment was Patricio Milmo, son-in-law of the powerful border governor Santiago Vidaurri, who more or less controlled the flow of commerce. Milmo learned that $16,000,000 in Confederate notes was en route through Matamoros to San Antonio to be shipped to Shreveport, and he seized the money in December 1863 as payment for the missing cotton. McKinney and Devine traveled the long hard road to Eagle Pass and Monterrey and within two weeks found a face-saving solution acceptable to all. McKinney and Devine promised that cotton to cover the value of the missing shipment would be delivered immediately and the Confederate notes were released.[9]

This promise led to McKinney's economic ruin. When he and the judge reached Eagle Pass on their return trip, there was no cotton waiting to be sent to Mexico. The pair returned home by March, then Devine went to the Confederate headquarters in Shreveport while Mac traveled to state headquarters in Houston to discover what was happening to the cotton that had supposedly been allocated to Milmo. In September, Mac complained to Guy

Bryan at Kirby Smith's headquarters in Shreveport that as soon as McKinney gathered cotton for Milmo, Confederate military agents in Texas seized it. Moreover, Mac reported fraud at every level until he finally gave up. He told Bryan that his accusations did no good and only caused him more trouble.[10]

McKinney owed almost $17,000 to neighborhood cotton planters John H. Pope, John Caldwell, T. P. Washington, and A. W. Moore, whose crops had been seized by Maj. Simeon Hart, the San Antonio quartermaster. McKinney felt personally responsible, and in March 1866, mortgaged his ranch, 100 cattle, and a jack and 150 jennets to the four men but reserved the right to use them until the creditors foreclosed. The nighmare continued and on December 27, 1867, Mac asked former Governor Pease, also a unionist, who had recently been appointed governor by Gen. Phillip Sheridan, for help. Pease had once worked as clerk for McKinney and Williams at Quintana. Mac tried to reconstruct a memorandum from memory because the books of Raymond, McKinney and Furman had been lost. McKinney had been able to pay over $16,000 in cotton, bagging, rope, and coffee to settle the debt to the planters. Now he wanted recompense from the state because he believed Major Hart had used the cotton destined for Milmo illegally.[11]

Another economic blow was the looting of McKinney's warehouse in Austin. When word reached Austin that the war had ended, Confederate troops in Texas began ransacking government storehouses because they had not received their pay. In Austin a combination of disgruntled soldiers and a mob stormed various warehouses in May, including McKinney's. Forty-six Travis County men and some sixty or seventy others from surrounding areas stole bagging, rope, kegs of horseshoes, and other items that McKinney valued at $8,000 in gold. Mac knew the identity of many of the looters and asked the District Court to charge them.[12] It appears from Mac's continued monetary distress that he received no redress for this incident or relief from the state concerning the Mexican cotton loss.

The McKinney household and neighborhood changed after the war. Eighty-five-year- old Eleanor McKinney died on July 18,

1865, and the family buried her in the Walker Austin cemetery near Cottonmouth Creek. Less than two months later Walker Austin died. The Austin cemetery may also hold the remains of Eleanor McKinney's sister Elizabeth Givens, who died about 1870. James and Elvira McKinney already had suffered several losses. In 1856 their oldest daughter Eleanor, age seventeen, died of scarlet fever in town at the Austin Collegiate Female Institute that had been founded two years earlier, and their fourteen-year-old son and a one-year-old infant died on Onion Creek, probably of the same disease. Another infant died in 1859; all seem to have been buried on the homesite. James and Elvira lived on their homestead until 1874 when she died of pneumonia and was buried in Oakwood Cemetery in town.

Tax records reveal how disastrous the Civil War was to Mac's financial condition. In 1866 the Travis County tax collector assessed McKinney for only forty horses, sixty cattle, and less than one hundred sheep, quite a contrast with pre-war years. In a poignant letter to Albert Sidney Johnston's son six years later, McKinney reluctantly admited their reduced circumstances and his own poor health: "My wife frequently has her own cooking & washing to do besides give much of her attention to our stock." He added that in spite of their changed lifestyle, she never was in low spirits and did not complain.[14] Anna, twenty years younger than Mac and raised by a widowed mother who was forced into becoming a teacher, could cope with the challenge.

By 1870, age and financial problems slowed down the once-vigorous McKinney. According to family lore he suffered with Bright's disease, an inflammation of the kidneys. Wanting to provide for Anna, McKinney swallowed his pride and composed a rambling petition to the state legislature in 1871 describing the losses of McKinney and Williams in 1835 and 1836 and how the firm had not been repaid in full. When a legislator questioned his long delay, the independent old man replied, "I have not especially needed it here-to-fore and was I in the enjoyment of good health, I would rather go to work to make the amount than ask it, though just, and doubly due." All he requested was the interest for the past twenty-five years, about $17,000, to be paid annually to himself and his wife as long as they lived. Many prominent old-timers endorsed the request but Attorney General William Alexander, an appointee of Republican Governor E. J. Davis, ruled that the petition required a two-thirds vote in each house (both in the hands of the Republicans), which defeated the bill.[15]

In the presidential election in November 1872, the revitalized Texas Democrats supported Horace Greeley over incumbent Republican President U. S. Grant; they also also elected their candidates for Congress and secured a majority in the state legislature. This Democratic victory also signaled the end of Republican rule in the gubernatorial race the following year. Mac resubmitted his petition during the next session of the legislature and the Senate Committee on the Public Debt unanimously passed the bill on May 28, 1873, recommending that the $16,942.80 in interest be paid semi-annually. The victory was hollow, however, because there were no funds.[16]

Four months later McKinney died at home at 2 a.m. on October 5, 1873. Austinites rallied to give McKinney a funeral befitting a pioneer Texan who had contributed so much to the Republic and state. Twenty citizens met in the mayor's office to plan the ceremonies, which took place the following day at 1 p.m. Friends and relatives accompanied the horse-drawn hearse from Onion Creek to the ferries on the Colorado River where the formal funeral procession formed at the foot of Congress Avenue. As the cortege made its way up the street to the Capitol, all the bells in the city tolled the usual somber peals. An honor guard of cadets from the Texas Military Institute and its band led the way followed by the appointed pallbearers, family and friends, heads of departments of the state government, and veterans of the Texas army and navy. Following the offical mourners were citizens on foot, in carriages, and on horseback, with volunteer firemen bringing up the rear. Several important figures spoke from the Capitol steps and Mac's longtime friend Judge Benjamin C. Franklin from Galveston and Brazoria delivered the eulogy followed by Dr. H. W. Dodge of the Baptist church. From the Capitol the procession moved east to Oakwood Cemetery for interment.[17]

Not long after Mac's death, James McKinney's wife, Elvira, died and he moved into town with a new wife who was a

Margaret Ann Taylor Lowry, grandniece of Thomas McKinney, c. 1891. *Photograph courtesy Texas State Library and Archives Commision.*

divorced Givens cousin. Anna remained at the ranch for a few years with Mac's great-niece Margaret Ann "Mag" Taylor and her husband, Robert W. Lowry. Mag had lived with the McKinneys in 1870 before she married in 1872, and the couple remained near the stone ranch house to help Mac and Anna. The three Lowry children, Anna McKinney, Reynolds K., and Mary N., were born there between 1874 and 1879. Lowry, a graduate engineer, supported his family by teaching in private schools and the state blind school plus dairy farming on a tract Mag had received from Mac. Anna sold a number of small tracts to kinsmen including the Lowrys, but in 1885 she sold most of the ranch property and the house to James W. Smith. He owned a large farm near Bluff Springs that he worked with the help of his son Felix; within a few years they acquired the remaining parcels of the McKinney land.[18] The Smiths worked their acreage with a number of black tenants, and some of those families lived in the old stone house. It was James W. Smith's grandchildren who donated the 682-acre scenic portion of the old ranch property to Texas Parks and Wildlife in 1974 for a state park so that others could enjoy its unique beauty.

In 1889 Anna lived in Austin at 2001 Whittis with longtime friends Albert Pickens Blocker and his wife, Cornelia. Blocker had been with Mac when he died and had prepared him for burial. By 1891 Anna lived alone near Guadalupe and Twentieth Street, and later on East Twelfth Street. A few days before Christmas 1896, Anna, age seventy-seven, hitched her horse, Bluebell, to her buggy and drove out to the small Lowry farm on Onion Creek. Two days after Christmas Anna went to bed early, and when the family looked in on her she was dead. In a strange way, her death at the Lowry house almost fulfilled her often expressed wish that she could die at her old home. In her will written in 1892 she left her piano, table silver, Bluebell, and the buggy to schoolteacher Anna McKinney Lowry, who was always called "Mac." Other personal items were specified for family and friends. When she wrote the will, Anna had $8,000, but how much of this remained four years later is unknown. She had set aside $300 for her own burial to be "like my husband—no better."[19] She lies next to him in Oakwood Cemetery east of the Capitol.

This pioneer pair who settled on Onion Creek invited many others to share their lifestyle during their years at the ranch. It is fitting that the nucleus of their homesite has been preserved so that visitors more than a century later can continue to enjoy the environs.

5.
THE ONION CREEK
COMMUNITY: A BRIEF LOOK

THE MCKINNEY RANCH became a community during the 1850s when kinsmen, friends, and employees bought or were given parcels of land. Besides the white horse trainer, Mac and James had a sufficient number of blacks who worked the land and animals. But McKinney most likely recruited Hispanic hands, probably in South Texas or around San Antonio, to care for the sheep and goats. The stacked stone fences also suggest Hispanic workmanship. After the Civil War at least one Mexican family and one black man acquired small tracts along Onion Creek within the area of the park. Lazaro Garza and his family lived on twenty-five acres on the south side of Williamson Creek near the jennet pasture while black Bob Holman had a cabin and field nearby though no deed indicates ownership. Garza was listed in the area in the 1870 census but not Bob.[1] Who these men were and what they did for McKinney remains unknown.

Tracing the McKinney blacks and their descendants is challenging and frustrating. One black family that descended from Daniel Alexander settled at Pilot Knob and had an oral tradition that Daniel had come to Texas with James P. McKinney. A deed record shows that Mac deeded a young slave named Daniel and his mother Ceny to James. While some former slaves adopted the last name of their former masters after 1865, others chose different surnames. Anna and Mac had a slave named Charley; this may the "colored" Charles McKinney who married "colored" Mary Jane

The McKinney home near Onion Creek, 1943. *Photograph by Reynolds K. Lowry, courtesy Texas State Library and Archives Commission.*

McKinney in Travis County in 1866.[2] The date of the marriage so soon after emancipation and with the same last names suggests that perhaps they were a couple before 1865 and wanted to legally establish their relationship under the new order.

A little more is known about black residents who lived in the old McKinney residence around the turn of the century. Charlie Johns, an eighty-year-old resident of Pilot Knob in 1974 when the archaeological investigation was under way in the park, shared his knowledge about the place after the turn of the century when his father was a tenant of the Smith family. He was one of ten children, born about 1885, whose grandfather had been a slave. His father grew cotton and vegetables and kept a few cows. As a boy, Charlie used the Smiths' work mules to haul water from Onion Creek up the hill for the livestock, but the family used water from the cistern for drinking. The house needed many repairs by the time Johns family left in the 1920s, but Charlie recalled that other black families occupied the house, some without permission. James E. "Pete" Smith, grandson of purchaser James W. Smith, believed the Johns were the last tenant farmers to live in the old house.[3] He may have been unaware that during the depression of the 1930s many families, black and white, were destitute and would have welcomed any kind of shelter.

The old stone house stood vacant and had been vandalized when Reynolds Lowry went out to take snapshots about 1943. At this time he was employed at the Austin Chamber of Commerce and was the last of his family in Austin. Neither he nor his sister Mac had married, and during the hard times of the 1930s they had to sell the McKinney silver to survive and even lost the home they had inherited. Following the death of his sister in 1936, Reynolds, in his sixties, devoted himself to preserving McKinney history. Saddened by the junk littering the yard, the high weeds, and the deteriorating wooden porches that someone had partially enclosed on the west ends, he must have described it to friends. According to Lowry, and this is open to question, Abner Pickens Blocker Jr.—former trail driver and rancher—went out the next day and set the place on fire.[4] Born on the nearby Blocker ranch in 1856 and well acquainted with the McKinneys, Ab—or Reynolds—must have decided that the old worn-out house deserved a decent funeral.

For thirty years the ruins remained a curiosity in the remote field until the Smith grandchildren deeded the land to Texas Parks and Wildlife in order that others could enjoy the scenic site and study the the evidence left by those who crossed the ancient ford.

NOTES

CHAPTER 1

1. Michael McEachern and Ronald W. Ralph, "Archeological Investigations at the Thomas F. McKinney Homestead . . ."*Bulletin of the Texas Archeological Society,* 52 (1980), 20-21 reviews past excavations; William C. Foster, *Spanish Expeditions into Texas, 1639-1768* (Austin: University of Texas Press, 1995), 60, 100, 101, 117, 191, 150, 168, 159.

2. For an explanation of these eleven-league grants see Margaret Swett Henson, *Samuel May Williams: Early Texas Entrepreneur* (College Station: Texas A&M University Press, 1976), 45-47.

3. S. F. Austin to Samuel M. Williams, May 8, 1832; May 31, 1833, in *The Austin Papers,* ed. Eugene C. Barker (3 vols; Washington, D. C.: U. S. Government Printing Office, 1924-1928), II, 771, 983; (Del Valle 10 leagues) General Land Office of Texas, 699:457 or see Virginia H. Taylor, *The Spanish Archives of the General Land Office of Texas* (Austin: Lone Star Press, 1974), apppendix listing all grants, 248; Travis County deed record, B, 51; 26,230.

CHAPTER 2

1. McKinney Family Bible. Thomas F. and James P. McKinney Papers, Center for American History, University of Texas at Austin, (hereafter CAH); Angela Morgan Burton, *Nellie B.: Tales of a Texan* (Prairie Valley, Kans.: The Squire Publishers, Inc., 1970), offers additional and sometimes differing genealogical material about family members; Cumberland County, Va., Court Order Book, I, 176; deed record, II, 54, III, 234, 272; Lunenburg County, Va., deed record, 10, 292; Charlotte County, Va., deed record 5, 106; Mercer County, Ky., deed record, 2, 398-99; Mercer County tax rolls, 1792, 1795, microfilm, Clayton Genealogical Library (Houston Public Library). For McKinney's father as a hunter see William S. Bryan and Robert Rose, *A History of the Pioneer Families of Missouri* (St. Louis: Bryan, Brand & Co., 1876), 354.

2. McKinney family lore about Mac's journey matches events of the second Cooper undertaking. See sketch of Mac provided by his brother James in the 1870s

in Charles W. Hayes, *History of the Island and the City of Galveston* (1879; reprint, Austin: Jenkins Garrett Press, 1974), 816-17; the Huguenot immigrant Subletts intermarried with the Chastains, one of whom married Charles McKinney, genealogical material in possession of author; for Sublett see Walter P. Webb, et al. (eds.), *The Handbook of Texas* (2 vols. plus supplement; Austin: Texas State Historical Association, 1952), II, 683, says Sublett was baptized in Durango; Sublett genealogical material in possession of author; Cooper advertisement in Missouri *Intelligencer*, May 13, June 17, 1823 in Thomas Becknell, "The Journals of Capt. Thomas Becknell . . . to Santa Fe . . .," *Missouri Historical Review*, 4 (Jan., 1910), 69-71; Max L. Moorehead, *New Mexico's Royal Road: Trade and Travel on the Chihuahua Trail* (Norman: University of Oklahoma Press, 1958), 62-64; R. L. Duffus, *The Santa Fe Trail*, (New York: 1930), 81.

3. Hayes, *History of Galveston*, 816.

4. Taylor, *The Spanish Archives*, 220.

5. 1828 Nacogdoches census, Robert Bruce Blake Research Collection Transcripts (93 vols., ca.1958, CAH), XVII, 45, 75; Virginia Eisenhour, "The Fabulous Enterpriser: Letters of Michel B. Menard," (n.p., n.d.), 2-3, copy in possession of author.

6. T. F. McKinney to S. M. Williams, Nov. 11, 1839; Certificate of Character, Nov. 11, 1839, Samuel May Williams Papers, Rosenberg Library, Galveston.

7. United States Eighth Census (1860), Travis County, Texas, 4th pct. no. 232, slave schedule, microfilm, Clayton Library; also in Alice Duggan Gracy and Emma Gene Seal Gentry (comps.), *Travis County, Texas: The Five Schedules of the 1860 Federal Census* (Austin: privately published, 1967), 65; Galveston County, Texas, deed record, C, 97; F, 222; Galveston County tax roll, 1841-1846, microfilm, Clayton Library; United States Seventh Census (1850), Galveston County, Texas, no. 652, population schedule, ibid.; Hayes, *History of Galveston*, 307.

8. Extract from testimony of T. F. McKinney about the Sanchez grant 1830, transcribed in R. B. Blake Transcripts, 7:608; "Personal Recollection," L. W. Groce to his son, Groce Family Papers, CAH; Groce mortgage to McKinney, May 24, 1831, Jared E. Groce document, Daughters of the Republic of Texas Library, San Antonio; Thomas F. McKinney to G. W. Smyth, Apr. 27, June 22, Dec. 5, 1831, George W. Smyth Collection, CAH; "Robber," Charles Adams Gulick Jr., et al. (eds.), *The Papers of Mirabeau Buonaparte Lamar*, (6 vols.; Austin: Von Boeckmann-Jones Co., 1927), IV, pt 1, 244-45; Hayes, *History of Galveston*, 817.

9. Henson, *Samuel May Williams*, 50; J. P. Bryan (ed.), *Mary Austin Holley: The Texas Diary, 1835-1838* (Austin: University of Texas Press, 1965), 13, 18, 23, 29, 60.

10. Brazoria *Texas Republican*, June 20, 1835; Bryan (ed.), *Mary Austin Holley*, 23; Margaret Swett Henson, *Lorenzo de Zavala: The Pragmatic Idealist* (Fort Worth: Texas Christian University Press, 1996), 78-81.

11. Brazoria *Texas Republican*, Oct. 31, 1835.

12. Henson, *Samuel May Williams*, 86; Brazoria County, probate record, James W. Fannin; T. F. McKinney to S. M. Williams, Nov. 6, 1838, Williams Papers; Betty Ballinger to Anna McKinney Lowry, Aug. 30, 1928, Lowry-McKinney Collection, Texas State Archives.

13. T. F. McKinney to S. M. Williams, Mar. 23, Apr. 1834; Oct. 9, 1834, Williams Papers; Galveston County, deed record, B2, 272-76; *Documents . . . Title to the Town Site on Galveston Island . . .* (1837), Galveston City Company Papers, CAH.

14. Henson, *Samuel May Williams*, 94-95, 115.

15. Sarah Williams to S. M. Williams, Oct. 24, 1838, Williams Papers; T. F. McKinney to S. M. Williams, Nov. 11, 1838, Thomas F. McKinney Papers, CAH; William Fairfax Gray, *From Virginia to Texas, 1835: The Diary of Col. Wm. F. Gray* (Houston: The Fletcher Young Publishing Co., 1965), 210; Lucy B. Jones to Mrs. W. H. Jack, Jack Family Papers, Rosenberg Library.

16. T. F. McKinney to S. M. Williams, Nov. 11, 1838, Thomas F. McKinney Papers, CAH; Lucy B. Jones to Laura Jack, May 7, 1842, Jack Family Papers; Margaret Swett Henson, *The Samuel May Williams Home: The Life and Neighborhood of an Early Galveston Entrepreneur* (Austin: Texas State Historical Association, 1992), 12-17, 27-35.

17. Galveston County deed record, A:570; Mrs. E. M. Gibbs to Marty Smith, Oct. 4, 1841, Rosenberg Library, Galveston, manuscript 24-0006; Houston *Morning Star*, July 16, 1842; Minutes Galveston District Court, B:153; Galveston County, marriage record, A:38; William H. Sandusky, *Plan of the City of Galveston, Texas*, 1845 (lithograph, 27½ x 37½ inches, Rosenberg Library) shows the McKinney house and others.

18. The United States Seventh Census (1850), Brazoria County, Texas, population schedule 147 lists Nancy with widow Laura Jack, as well as Nancy's two nieces and a nephew from Georgia. Nancy bought a home in 1852 (Brazoria County, deed record, L, 434) after Laura Jack moved to Galveston to live with her married daughter. United States Eighth Census (1860), Brazoria County, Texas, population schedule 420 shows Nancy as head of household with two nieces and a minister and son, boarders; Brazoria County, probate record no. 897 for Nancy McKinney notes no relatives in the county and states that on her deathbed in 1869, Nancy gave her homestead to the wife of a neighbor who had perhaps cared for her.

19. Malcolm D. McLean, *Fine Texas Horses: Their Pedigrees and Performance, 1830-1845* (Fort Worth: Texas Christian University Press, 1966), 21-29; Willis W. Pratt (ed.), *Galveston Island: Or, A Few Months Off the Coast of Texas: The Journal of Francis C. Sheridan, 1839-1840* (Austin: University of Texas Press, 1954), 50.

20. Pratt (ed.), *Galveston Island*, 30-31.

21. Patsy McDonald Spaw (ed.), *The Texas Senate, vol. 1, Republic to Civil War, 1836-1861* (College Station: Texas A&M University Press, 1990), 165-184.

22. Rhoda van Bibber Tanner Doubleday (ed.), *Journals of the Late Brevet Major Philip Norbourne Barbour. . . and His Wife* (New York: G. P. Putnam's Sons, 1936), 116. 118-21, 135, 139-40.

CHAPTER 3

1. Genealogy charts in possession of author and fragmented references to James in various legal documents and letters.

Neither T. F. McKinney nor his brother James intentionally preserved records for descendants or family; one almost feels they were destroyed. The first collector was Mattie Austin Hatcher, daughter of Walker Austin's youngest child, Charles Freeman (1851-1930) and Anna Pope Hague, who attended the University of Texas and as librarian and archivist there published the first biography of Mary Austin Holley in 1933. She gave small collections of McKinney and Austin documents to both the university library and the Austin Public Library in the early 1900s. Other fugitive McKinney documents have surfaced; some were collected by Reynolds Lowry and placed in the Texas State Archives in the 1940s.

2. Travis County deed record, C, 115; Paul H. Carlson, *Texas Woollybacks: The Range Sheep and Goat Industry* (College Station: Texas A&M University Press, 1982), 28-29; United States Seventh Census (1850) Travis County, Texas, agricultural and slave schedules, (microfilm, Clayton Library).

3. Travis County tax roll, 1848, (microflim: Clayton Library).

4. Petition of Thomas F. McKinney, printed copy to Committee on Public Debt, T. F. McKinney Papers, CAH; T. F. McKinney to S. M. Williams, Feb. 1856, Williams Papers.

5. E. W. Taylor to Samuel May Williams, June 21, 1848 (lumber), Williams Papers; Galveston *Weekly News* Oct. 18, Nov. 10, 1848, Mar. 16, 1849 (arrivals from New Orleans); Galveston *Weekly News*, Dec. 22, 1848 (canal); Galveston County Commissioner Court Minutes, Aug. 3, 1846, Nov 20, 1849, Feb. 19, 1855; Aug. 18, 1857; Apr. 11, 1866.

6. T. F. McKinney to S. M. Williams, Nov. 23, 1849,Williams Papers; Michael McEachern and Ronald W. Ralph, "Appendix D: Texas Parks and Wildlife Excavations at the McKinney Homestead," *Bulletin of the Texas Archeological Society*, 51 (1980), 159; Austin *Texas State Gazette*, July 10, 1852; Houston *Telegraph and Texas Register*, July 16, 1852.

7. McEachern and Ralph, "Archaeological Investigations at the McKinney Homestead," 35-45 includes the 1943 photographs by Reynolds Lowry cited to the CAH (perhaps in error), which in 1996 were available at the Austin History Center and in the Lowry-McKinney Collection at the Texas State Archives.

8. Items listed in Anna G. McKinney's will, Feb. 11, 1892, filed Jan. 16, 1897, no. 2047, Travis County probate records; folder about the Sir Archy painting in the Lowry-McKinney Collection.

9. United States Eighth Census (1860), Travis County, Texas, slave schedule, microfilm, Clayton Library, also in Gracy and Gentry (comps.), *Travis County . . . the 1860 Federal Census*, 65; Reynolds Lowry map and notes, Lowry-McKinney Collection; McEachern and Ralph, "Archaeological Investigations at the McKinney Homestead," 51, 14, 95, 27.

10. Lowry map and notes, Lowry-McKinney Collection.

11. Betty Ballinger to Anna McKinney Lowry, Aug. 30, 1928; Reynolds Lowry notes, Lowry-McKinney Collection.

12. Mary Starr Barkley, *History of Travis County and Austin, 1839-1899* (Austin: The Steck Company, 1963), 159, 257, 265-67; Galveston *Weekly News*, June 23, Sept. 8, 1857; Shaw (ed.), *The Texas Senate*, 275-300.

13. Walker Austin's accounts with Austin merchants, fall 1857, Walker Austin Collection, CAH; document signed by McKinney and other heirs related to moving

slave property from Missouri, Apr. 15, 1858, McKinney (Thos. F.) Family Papers, Texas State Archives; United States Eighth Census (1860), Travis County, Texas, population schedule, no. 221, 230, 232; Mildred P. Mayhall, "Newton Curd Givens," in Ron Tyler, et al. (eds.), *New Handbook of Texas* (6 vols; Austin: Texas State Historical Association, 1996), III, 176; hereafter cited as NHOT.

CHAPTER 4

1. United States Eighth Census (1860), Travis County, Texas, agricultural and slave schedules for no. 228 (JPM) and no. 232 (TFM); *A Pictorial History of Austin, Travis County, Texas' Black Community, 1839-1920* (Austin: Delta Sigma Theta Sorority, Inc., c. 1976), 34; James P. McKinney to Walker Austin, Aug. 30, 1838, Thomas F. McKinney Papers, CAH.

2. United States Eighth Census (1860), Travis County, Texas, agricultural and slave schedules for no. 237; John G. Johnson, "Austin State Hospital" in NHOT, I, 314.

3. Edd Miller, "Josephus Murray Steiner" in NHOT, VI, 81; Thomas W. Cutrer, "Ripley Allen Arnold," ibid., I, 253; Reynolds Lowry Notes, Lowry-McKinney Collection, Texas State Archives; F. S. Stockdale to Dr. Steiner, May 11, 1866, Albert Sidney Burleson Collection, CAH.

4. T. F. McKinney to Guy M. Bryan, Nov. 22, 1860, quoted in Walter L. Buenger, *Secession and the Union in Texas* (Austin: University of Texas Press, 1984), 123 (quotations).

5. Buenger, *Secession and the Union*, 174-176; Randolph B. Campbell, *Sam Houston and the American Southwest* (New York: Harper Collins College Publications, 1993), 156.

6. Walker Austin to A. J. Rose, July 7, 1860, Walker Austin Papers, CAH; also see Buenger, *Secession and the Union*, 176-177.

7. Paula Mitchell Marks, *Turn Your Eyes Toward Texas: Pioneers Sam and Mary Maverick* (College Station: Texas A&M University Press, 1989), 235; Ronnie C. Tyler, *Santiago Vidaurri and the Southern Confederacy* (Austin: Texas State Historical Association, 1973), 105: T. F. McKinney to E. M. Pease, Dec. 27, 1867, Thomas F. McKinney file, Austin History Center.

8. Tyler, *Santiago Vidaurri*, 98-128, particularly 108-109, 113, 119.

9. Ibid., 122-127.

10. T. J. Devine to T. F. McKinney, Mar. 17, 1864, Thomas J. Devine letters (transcripts), CAH; also see Mary Owen Meredith, "The Life and Work of Thomas Jefferson Devine," (M. A. thesis, University of Texas, 1930), 59-66; T. F. McKinney to Guy M. Bryan, Nov. 2, 1864, Guy M. Bryan Papers, CAH.

11. T. F. McKinney to Gov. E. M. Pease, Dec. 27, 1867, Thomas F. McKinney file, Austin History Center; Travis County deed record (mortgage to John H. Pope, John Caldwell, T. P. Washington, A. W. Moore), Q, 419-421,

12. D. W. C. Baker, *A Texas Scrapbook* (1875: reprint, Austin: Texas State Historical Association, 1991), 348-350; petition of Thomas F. McKinney to Judge of Second Judicial District, Nov. 2, 1865, copy in Thomas F. McKinney file, Austin History Center.

13. Eleanor McKinney obituary, Austin *Southern Intelligencer*, July 18, 1865; Thelma Rodgers Cook (Mrs. Carroll H. Cook, descendant of Walker Austin), "Notes on the Austin Cemetery," in author's possession; other genealogical material in possession of author.

14. Travis County tax roll, 1866, microfilm, Texas State Library; T. F. McKinney to Preston Johnston, Dec. 28, 1872, Julia Lee Sinks papers, CAH.

15. Petition of T. F. McKinney, Senate Bill 162, file box 128 (1940s), copy in Lowry-McKinney Collection.

16. Ibid.

17. Austin *Daily Democratic Statesman*, Oct. 3, 1873.

18. Advertisements for 1,081 acres, Austin *Daily Democratic Statesman*, June 9, 1878; Travis County deed records, 57:438; 54:879; 67:28, 30; 75:581.

19. Austin city directories, 1881-1882, 1883, 1885-1886, 1889-1890; Reynolds Lowry notes, folder 2, Lowry-McKinney Collection; Anna G. McKinney will, Travis County Probate no. 2047, copy in Lowry-McKinney collection.

CHAPTER 5

1. Lazaro Garza, Travis County deed record, R, 195, 102, 382; United States Ninth Census (1870), Travis County, Texas, population schedule 119; Reynolds Lowry map and notes, Lowry-McKinney Collection.

2. *A Pictorial History of Austin, Travis County, Texas' Black Community*, 34-35; Travis County deed record, C, 115; will of Thomas F. and Anna G. McKinney, Jan. 25, 1864, Travis County deed record, Q, 115, typescript copy in Lowry-McKinney Collection; Ceny and Daniel mentioned in Travis County deed record, C, 115.

3. McEachern and Ralph, "Archaeological Investigations at the McKinney Homestead," 51, 18-19.

4. Reynolds Lowry notes, Lowry-McKinney Collection.